A CATHOLIC
PRAYER BOOK

Revised by Amette Ley

*All booklets are published
thanks to the generosity of the supporters
of the Catholic Truth Society*

Contents

All rights reserved. First published 2014 by The Incorporated Catholic Truth Society, 42-46 Harleyford Road London SE11 5AY. Tel: 020 7640 0042. © 2014 The Incorporated Catholic Truth Society. www.ctsbooks.org

ISBN 978 1 86082 927 7

~ Introduction to Prayer ~

Scripture and Christian Prayer

Prayer is completely bound up with our human history and our history of salvation. In the Old Testament we hear of a prayerful relationship between God and man even before the covenant with Abraham when men such as Enoch "walked with God" and Noah, who had an "upright and undivided" heart. God has always called people to respond to him in prayer.

Abraham

Abraham is one such man, and God begins to reveal the nature of prayer through him. *The Catechism of the Catholic Church*, CCC 2570 notes what is revealed: Abraham's heart is entirely submissive to the Word - he is "walking with God". (*Gn* 12) From this submissiveness of heart comes his obedience - he does what God asks. Having an attentive heart and making decisions according to God's will is the essence of prayer. The words we use only have value in relation to this. Alone they are nothing. We don't hear anything about Abraham's words to start with; his prayer is expressed first by deeds. We hear that he constructs an altar to the Lord at each stage of his journey. It's after this that we hear Abraham's words to God. He has won a battle, been blessed by Melchizedek (*Gn* 14) and has given tithes of what he won to God - now he wonders what God's promises to him really mean. "'Lord God, what can this gift of yours be?' And God answers: 'Look up at the sky, and count, if you can, the stars in it; your race, like these, shall be numberless.' So Abram put his faith in God, and it was reckoned virtue in him." (*Gn* 15:2, 5-6) We begin to have an idea here of what the CCC calls the "drama of prayer" right from the beginning: the test of faith in the fidelity of God.

Old Testament Figures

Many other Old Testament characters reveal more to us about prayer. We hear of Jacob, who wrestles all night with a mysterious figure, showing that prayer is a struggle and that perseverance in prayer is necessary.

There is Moses, who meets God in the burning bush and shows that the place where God comes to us is holy. Later the Ark of the Covenant and the Temple will become this holy place. "Moses also learns how to pray: he balks, makes excuses, above all questions: and it is in response to his question that the Lord confides his ineffable name, which will be revealed through his mighty deeds." (CCC 2575)

We hear that Samuel learns how to listen to God in the Temple at Shiloh and is guided by his mother Hannah and the priest Eli. We find David, the shepherd-king who trusts in God, sins and repents, and prays on behalf of his people. The psalms, inspired by the Holy Spirit, show this mixture of praise, blessing and repentance and they are a model for the prayer of the people, even today.

Solomon, David's son, builds the Temple as a dwelling place for God and as a place of prayer. (*Mt* 21:13) "The king lifts his hands toward heaven and begs the Lord, on his own behalf, on behalf of the entire people, and of the generations yet to come, for the forgiveness of their sins and for their daily needs, so that the nations may know that He is the only God and that the heart of his people may belong wholly and entirely to him." (CCC 2580)

However, Elijah and the prophets show that although the Temple rituals are ways of prayer, they must be matched by inner conversion of heart.

Of all these Old Testament characters and all they have to teach us about prayer, it is the experience of Moses which the Catechism highlights as the way to approach Jesus "as Moses approached the burning bush: first to contemplate him in prayer, then to hear how he teaches us to pray, in order to know how he hears our prayer." (CCC 2598)

The suggestion of the Catechism that we approach God in this way is not one we always find in books on prayer. Sometimes we are presented with a kind of hierarchy of prayer; first vocal prayer, either spontaneous or formulaic; then mental prayer which can be meditative or contemplative, the highest form of prayer. The Catechism itself gives this order and description later in the section on prayer. But here, the concept is a simpler one. Contemplation is where we start. We don't have to work up to it as some kind of spiritual achievement; we go straight in there and have a look, as Moses did with the burning bush. Of course, if we are not living in obedience of action, as Moses was, and not willing, as he was, to approach God, we will be in the wrong place to start with - we may not notice our burning bush. But once we have stopped to contemplate, we need to listen. And maybe, like Moses, the first thing we will hear is our name, spoken in love by the God who made us.

Mary

In the New Testament, the most significant example of prayer after Jesus himself is that of Our Lady. As Daughter of Zion, she encapsulates in herself the whole life of prayer of Israel.

Like Abraham and those before him, she is "walking with God"; her heart is submissive to him and she is obedient in her actions which are reflected in her words.

"Behold the handmaid of the Lord - be it done unto me according to thy word." When she does speak, we hear her yearning to understand how this shall be, just as Abraham wondered how it would be that he would have a descendant. She too is part of the "drama of prayer".

Like Jacob, she struggles to understand. How shall this be, as I am a virgin? Like Moses, Mary contemplates God. She is in the right place, obediently living her life, and she does not turn away when she sees and hears what must seem impossible. Like Moses, she hears her new 'name' and her task, and like him she remains in God's presence and listens and responds.

Like Samuel, she has learned in the Temple to listen to God - tradition tells us she was presented there at an early age, and even if this should not be completely accurate, the memory of the Church is connecting her from the first to the Temple. She is able, from her submissiveness of heart and her obedience in action, to respond to God's call.

Like David and Solomon, she prays in the name of the people in her Magnificat and her prayer becomes a model for the prayer of the People of God. Her Magnificat "is the song both of the Mother of God and of the Church; the song of the Daughter of Zion and of the new People of God; the song of thanksgiving for the fullness of graces poured out in the economy of salvation and the song of the 'poor' whose hope is met by the fulfilment of the promises made to our ancestors, 'to Abraham and to his posterity forever.'" (CCC 2619)

And with Elijah and the prophets, she observes the Temple rituals, but she surely understands that true prayer is the worship of the heart.

The Teaching of Jesus on Prayer

The Gospels also tell us how and when Jesus prayed, often alone and at night; St Luke's Gospel emphasises this in particular. He did not set aside time in the day when he was needed by others; he took his own time, the time of the night, in order to pray.

The Catechism points us particularly to the priestly prayer of Jesus, given in the Fourth Gospel and shows us that when Jesus prays, he is already teaching us how to pray. (CCC 2607) But he also taught his followers specifically how to pray in the 'Our Father'. "Like a wise teacher he takes hold of us where we are and leads us progressively toward the Father." We are then drawn into prayer with the Son to the Father in the power of the Holy Spirit.

Jesus insists on genuine conversion of heart, true prayer, sincere repentance. This enables the heart to pray in faith in a real adherence to the Father. This prayer of faith is not just words, but must make the heart disposed to do the will of the Father. Jesus encourages us, as sons, to be bold in prayer. He himself, when he prays, often gives thanks to the Father even before he has received the gifts. (E.g. *Jn* 11:41)

Jesus calls for conversion and faith, but also for watchfulness in prayer; prayer, as Jacob knew, is a battle and we have to be watchful so that we don't fall into temptation. Prayer is to be in the name of Jesus once he has returned to the Father, because he is the Way, Truth and Life - this was a new concept for God's people. And there is another Counsellor to be with us - the Spirit of Truth.

So we pray in the name of Jesus, to him as Lord and God, and with him to the Father. "St Augustine wonderfully summarises the three dimensions of Jesus's prayer: 'He prays for us as our priest, prays in us as our Head, and is prayed to by us as our God.'" (CCC 2616)

~ Preparing for Prayer ~

Jesus, grant me grace to fix my mind on thee,
especially in time of prayer,
when I directly converse with thee.

Stop the motions of my wandering head,
and the desires of my unstable heart;
suppress the power of my spiritual enemies,
who endeavour at that time to draw my mind from
heavenly thoughts, to many vain imaginations.

So shall I, with joy and gratitude,
look on thee as my deliverer from all the evils
I have escaped; and as my benefactor for all the good
I have ever received, or can hope for.
I shall see that thou art my only good,
and that all other things are but means ordained
by thee to make me fix my mind on thee,
to make me love thee more and more,
and, by loving thee, to be eternally happy.
O beloved of my soul, take up all my thoughts here,
that my eyes, abstaining from vain and hurtful sights,
may become worthy to behold thee face to face
in thy glory for ever. Amen.

From the Jesus Psalter, written by Richard Whitford,
an English Bridgettine monk, in the sixteenth century.

It would be easier for a man to stop the stars in their rotation through the heavens, than for him to quiet his mind by human effort. But the same God who made the stars also made the mind, and he will quiet both in his own time. Until that Day, the stars must continue in their paths, and the human mind must be put to the active consideration of the mysteries of our faith. When God so wills to quiet the mind, let that man rejoice and be at peace, but may he recall that he then has a special obligation to perform many works of charity for his neighbour.

St Teresa of Avila

~ Beginnings ~

The Sign of the Cross

Christians begin their day, their prayers, and their activities with the sign of the cross. The sign of the cross strengthens us in our temptations and difficulties.

In nómine Patris, et Fílii, et Spíritus Sancti. Amen.
Per signum crucis de inimícis nostris líbera nos, Deus noster.

In the name of the Father, and of the Son, and of the Holy Spirit. Amen.
By the sign of the cross deliver us from our enemies, you who are our God.

The Lord's Prayer

This is the prayer which Jesus taught his apostles when they asked him to show them how to pray (see Mt 6:19 and Lk 11:24).

Pater noster, qui es in caelis, sanctificétur nomen tuum.
Advéniat regnum tuum.
Fiat volúntas tua, sicut in caelo et in terra.

Our Father, who art in heaven, hallowed be thy name.
Thy kingdom come;
Thy will be done on earth, as it is in heaven.

Panem nostrum quotidiánum da nobis hódie, et dimítte nobis débita nostra sicut et nos dimíttimus debitóribus nostris. Et ne nos indúcas in tentatiónem, sed líbera nos a malo. Amen.

Give us this day our daily bread, and forgive us our trespasses, as we forgive those who trespass against us, and lead us not into temptation, but deliver us from evil. Amen.

Glory be to the Father

The giving of glory and adoration to God is the basic duty of mankind, his creatures. In this form, called 'The little Doxology', it appears at the end of most psalms in the Divine Office.

Glória Patri, et Fílio, et Spirítui Sancto. Sicut erat in princípio et nunc et semper et in saecula saéculórum. Amen.

Glory be to the Father, and to the Son, and to the Holy Spirit. As it was in the beginning is now, and ever shall be, world without end. Amen.

Daily Dedication and the Morning Offering

It has long been the habit of many Catholics to dedicate their day to God as soon as they awake. Beginning with the sign of the cross, a simple prayer of trust in God places the whole day in his hands. It is important that we pray daily so that the relationship of prayer is sustained, and making a morning offering sets the whole day in the context of God's call to us and our response.

O Jesus, through the Immaculate Heart of Mary, I offer you my prayers, works, joys and sufferings of this day for all the intentions of Your Sacred Heart, in union with the Holy Sacrifice of the Mass throughout the world, in reparation for my sins, for the intentions of all my relatives and friends, and in particular for the intentions of the Holy Father. Amen.

For children

O my God, I offer you,
All that I think, or say, or do.
Help me give to you today
All my life, in every way,

The following prayer is also good to say at the start of the day and as any new venture begins.

L ord, be the beginning and end of all we do and say. Prompt our actions with your grace, and complete them with your all-powerful help. We ask this through Christ our Lord. Amen.

Formerly the collect for Ember Saturday in Lent, this prayer is now used on the Thursday after Ash Wednesday.

~ Morning Prayer ~

An order for Morning Prayer

V.   O Lord open our lips
R.   And we shall praise your name.

Glory be to the Father, and to the Son, and to the Holy Spirit, as it was in the beginning, is now and ever shall be, world without end. Amen. (Alleluia.)

A suitable hymn such as one of the following is said:

Transcendent God in whom we live,
The Resurrection and the Light,
We sing for you a morning hymn,
To end the silence of the night.

When early cock begins to crow,
And everything from sleep awakes,
New life and hope spring up again,
While out of darkness colour breaks.

Creator of all things that are,
The measure and the end of all,
Forgiving God, forget our sins,
And hear our prayer before we call.

Praise Father, Son and Holy Ghost,
Blest Trinity and source of grace,
Who call us out of nothingness,
To find in you our resting place.

⌒

Father, we praise thee, now the night is over;
   Active and watchful, stand we all before thee;
Singing, we offer, prayer and meditation;
Thus we adore thee.

Monarch of all things, fit us for thy mansions;
Banish our weakness, health and wholeness sending;
Bring us to heaven, where thy saints united
Joy without ending.

All holy Father, Son and equal Spirit,
Trinity blessèd, send us thy salvation;
Thine is the glory, gleaming and resounding
Through all creation.

⌒

O Christ, the Light of heaven
   And of the world true Light,
You come in all your radiance
To cleave the web of night.

May what is false within us
Before your truth give way,
That we may live untroubled
With quiet hearts this day.

May steadfast faith sustain us,
And hope made firm in you;
The love that we have wasted,
Oh God of love, renew.

Blest Trinity we praise you
In whom our quest will cease;
Keep us with you for ever
In happiness and peace.

Alone with none but thee, my God,
I journey on my way.
What need I fear when thou art near,
O King of night and day?
More safe am I within thy hand
than if a host should round me stand.

My destined time is known to thee,
and death will keep his hour;
did warriors strong around me throng,

they could not stay his power:
no walls of stone can man defend
when thou thy messenger dost send.

My life I yield to thy decree,
and bow to thy control
in peaceful calm, for from thine arm
no power can wrest my soul.
Could earthly omens e'er appal
a man that heeds the heavenly call?

The child of God can fear no ill,
his chosen dread no foe;
we leave our fate with thee, and wait
thy bidding when to go.
'Tis not from chance our comfort springs.'
thou art our trust, O King of kings.

One or more of the following psalms may be said:

Psalm 63

O God, you are my God, for you I long;
for you my soul is thirsting,
My body pines for you
like a dry, weary land without water.
So I gaze on you in the sanctuary
to see your strength and your glory.

For your love is better than life,
my lips will speak your praise.
So I will bless you all my life,
in your name I will lift up my hands.
My soul shall be filled as with a banquet,
my mouth shall praise you with joy.
On my bed I remember you.
On you I muse through the night
for you have been my help;
in the shadow of your wings I rejoice.
My soul clings to you;
your right hand holds me fast.

Glory be...

Psalm 149

Sing a new song to the Lord,
his praise in the assembly of the faithful.
Let Israel rejoice in its Maker,
let Sion's sons exult in their king.
Let them praise his name with dancing
and make music with timbrel and harp.

For the Lord takes delight in his people.
He crowns the poor with salvation.
Let the faithful rejoice in their glory,
shout for joy and take their rest.

Let the praise of God be on their lips
and a two-edged sword in their hand,
to deal out vengeance to the nations
and punishment on all the peoples;
to bind their kings in chains
and their nobles in fetters of iron;
to carry out the sentence preordained:
this honour is for all his faithful.

Glory be...

(Other psalms suitable for morning prayer include psalms 24, 67 & 100.)

Scripture Reading

You know what hour it is, how it is full time now for you to wake from sleep. The night is far gone, the day is at hand. Let us cast off the works of darkness and put on the armour of light; let us conduct ourselves becomingly as in the day.

(Rm 13:11b, 1213a)

Short Responsory

R. You are the Christ, Son of the living God. Have mercy on us. (Repeat.)

V. You are seated at the right hand of the Father.

R. You are the Christ, Son of the living God. Have mercy on us.

V. Glory be to the Father, and to the Son,
     and to the Holy Spirit.
R. You are the Christ, Son of the living God.
     Have mercy on us.

The Benedictus (Canticle of Zechariah)

This is a canticle from the Gospels - the prayer of praise spoken by Zechariah to praise God for the gift of his Son John (later known as John the Baptist). We acknowledge its importance by standing and making the sign of the cross.

Blessed be the Lord, the God of Israel!
He has visited his people and redeemed them.
He has raised up for us a mighty saviour
in the house of David his servant,
as he promised by the lips of holy men,
those who were his prophets from of old.

A saviour who would free us from our foes,
from the hands of all who hate us.
So his love for our fathers is fulfilled
and his holy covenant remembered.

He swore to Abraham our father to grant us,
that free from fear, and saved from the hands of our foes,
we might serve him in holiness and justice
all the days of our life in his presence.

As for you, little child,
you shall be called a prophet of God, the Most High.
You shall go ahead of the Lord
to prepare his ways before him.
To make known to his people their salvation
through forgiveness of all their sins,
the loving kindness of the heart of our God
who visits us like the dawn from on high.

He will give light to those in darkness,
those who dwell in the shadow of death,
and guide us into the way of peace.

Glory be...

Intercessions

V. Let us pray to Christ our Lord, the sun who enlightens all people:

R. Lord our Saviour, give us life!

V. We thank you for the gift of this new day.

R. Lord our Saviour, give us life!

V. May your Holy Spirit guide us to do your will.

R. Lord our Saviour, give us life!

V. Help us to manifest your love to all those we meet.

R. Lord our Saviour, give us life!

V. Renew in us your gifts, may we go forth in peace.

R. Lord our Saviour, give us life!

Our Father...

Concluding Prayer

Almighty God, you have given us this day;
strengthen us with your power
and keep us from falling into sin,
so that whatever we say, or think, or do,
may be in your service and for the sake of the kingdom.
We ask this through our Lord Jesus Christ your Son,
who lives and reigns in the unity of the Holy Spirit,
ever one God, world without end. Amen.
May the Lord bless us, keep us from all evil and bring
us to everlasting life.
Amen.

~ Prayers Throughout ~ the Day

Morning Prayer of St Francis

Lord, help me to live this day, quietly, easily;
to lean on your great strength, trustfully, restfully;
to wait for the unfolding of your will, patiently, serenely;
to meet others, peacefully, joyfully;
to face tomorrow, confidently, courageously.

Prayer of St Thérèse of Lisieux

My life is but an instant, a passing hour.
My life is but a day that escapes and flies away.
O my God! You know that to love you on earth
I only have today.

Lord, what does it matter if the future is gloomy?
To pray for tomorrow, oh no, I cannot!
Keep my heart pure, cover me with your shadow
Just for today.

O divine Pilot! whose hand guides me.
I'm soon to see you on the eternal shore.
Guide my little boat over the stormy waves in peace
Just for today.

Prayer of Abandonment

Father, I abandon myself into your hands;
   Do with me what you will.
Whatever you may do, I thank you;
I am ready for all, I accept all.
Let only your will be done in me and in all your creatures.
I wish no more than this, O Lord.
Into your hands I commend my soul:
I offer it to you with all the love of my heart,
for I love you, Lord, and so need to give myself,
to surrender myself into your hands without reserve
and with boundless confidence, for you are my Father.

Charles de Foucauld

St Patrick's Breastplate

I bind unto myself today,
   the power of God to hold and lead,
his eye to watch, his might to stay,
his ear to harken to my need:
the wisdom of my God to teach,
his hand to guide, his shield to ward;
the word of God to give me speech,
his heavenly host to be my guard.
Christ be with me,
Christ within me,

Christ behind me,
Christ before me,
Christ beside me,
Christ to win me,
Christ to comfort and restore me.
Christ beneath me,
Christ above me, Christ in quiet,
Christ in danger,
Christ in hearts of all that love me,
Christ in mouth of friend and stranger.

Prayer for Humility

Most humble Jesus, give me a share of your humility. Take from my heart everything that displeases you; convert it totally to you,
so that I may no longer will or desire
anything other than what you will.

St Alphonsus Ligouri

Prayer of Thanksgiving

We give you thanks for all your gifts, Almighty God, living and reigning
now and forever.
Amen.

Grace before meals

Bless us, O Lord, and these thy gifts which we are about to receive through thy bounty.
Through Christ our Lord.
Amen.

Thanksgiving after meals

We give thee thanks for all thy benefits, Almighty God,
who live and reign world without end. Amen.

May the souls of the faithful departed, through the mercy of God, rest in peace. Amen.

Prayers to our Guardian Angel

Angel sent by God to guide me, be my light and walk beside me; be my guardian and protect me; on the paths of life direct me.

Angel of God, my guardian dear, to whom God's love commits me here, ever this day (or night) be at my side, to light, to guard, to rule and guide. Amen.

Te Deum

You are God; we praise you; you are the Lord; we acclaim you; you are the eternal Father. All creation worships you. To you all angels, all the powers of heaven, cherubim and seraphim, sing in endless praise;

holy, holy, holy Lord, God of power and might, heaven and earth are full of your glory. The glorious company of apostles praise you. The noble fellowship of prophets praise you. The white-robed army of martyrs praise you. Throughout the world the holy Church acclaims you;

Father, of majesty unbounded, your true and only Son, worthy of all worship, and the Holy Spirit, advocate and guide. You, Christ, are the king of glory, the eternal Son of the Father. When you became man to set us free you did not spurn the Virgin's womb. You overcame the sting of death, and opened the kingdom of heaven to all believers. You are seated at God's right hand in glory. We believe that you will come, and be our judge. Come then, Lord and help your people, bought with the price of your own blood, and bring us with your saints to glory everlasting.

Save your people, Lord, and bless your inheritance. Govern and uphold them now and always. Day by day we bless you. We praise your name for ever. Keep us today, Lord, from all sin. Have mercy on us, Lord, have mercy. Lord, show us your love and mercy; for we put our trust in you. In you, Lord, is our hope; and we shall never hope in vain.

Written at the beginning of the fifth century,
perhaps by St Nicetas of Remesiana (335-415)

Act of Faith, Hope and Love

My God, I believe in you,
I trust in you,
I love you above all things,
with all my heart and mind and strength.
I love you because you are supremely
   good and worth loving;
and because I love you,
I am sorry with all my heart for offending you.
Lord, have mercy on me, a sinner.
Amen.

Come Holy Spirit

The first versicle and response are taken from the alleluia verse before the Gospel of Pentecost; the second versicle and response from the third antiphon for the Office of Readings on Pentecost and the prayer from the votive Mass of the Holy Spirit in the Roman Missal.

V.   Come, Holy Spirit, fill the hearts of your faithful
R.   And kindle in them the fire of your love.
V.   Send forth your Spirit and they shall be created
R.   And you will renew the face of the earth.
Let us pray.
Lord, by the light of your Holy Spirit
you have taught the hearts of your faithful.

In that same Spirit
help us to relish what is right
and always rejoice in your consolation.
We ask this through Christ our Lord.
R. Amen.

Prayer for Benefactors

Reward those who have been good to us
for the sake of your name,
O Lord and give them eternal life.
Amen.

Prayer of St Francis

Lord make me an instrument of your peace;
where there is hatred,
let me sow love;
where there is injury, pardon;
where there is discord, union;
where there is doubt, faith;
where there is despair, hope;
where there is darkness, light;
where there is sadness, joy;
O Divine Master, grant that I may not so much seek to
be consoled as to console,
to be understood as to understand, to be loved as to
love. For it is in giving that we receive.

It is in pardoning that we are pardoned,
and it is in dying that we are born to eternal life.
Amen.

Prayer for Final Perseverance

Our dear Redeemer,
relying on your promises,
because you are faithful, all-powerful and merciful,
we hope, through the merits of your Passion,
for the forgiveness of our sins,
perseverance until death in your grace;
and at length we hope, by your mercy,
to see and love you eternally in heaven.

St Alphonsus Ligouri

Prayer for Christian Unity

O Lord Jesus Christ,
when you were about to suffer,
you prayed for your disciples to the end of time,
that they might all be one,
as you are in the Father,
and the Father in you.
Look down in pity on the many divisions
among those who profess your faith and heal the
wounds which the pride of man and the craft of Satan
have inflicted on your people.

Break down the walls of separation which divide one party and denomination of Christians from another. Look with compassion on the souls who have been born in one or another of these various communions and bring them all into that one communion which you set up in the beginning: the One, Holy, Catholic and Apostolic Church.

John Henry Newman; adapted from
'Meditations and Devotions'

St Patrick's Prayer

I arise today, through the power of the Trinity, through the faith in threeness, through trust in the oneness of the Maker of the earth, and the Maker of heaven.

Prayer of St Richard

Praise be to thee, O Lord Jesus Christ,
For all the benefits which you have given us,
For all the pains and insults which you have borne for us.
O most merciful Redeemer, friend and brother,
May we see you more clearly, love you more dearly,
And follow you more nearly, day by day. Amen.

St Richard of Chichester (1198-1253)

Prayer of St Ignatius Loyola

Teach us Good Lord,
To serve you as you deserve,
To give and not to count the cost,
To fight and not to heed the wounds,
To toil and not to seek for rest,
To labour and not to ask for any reward,
Save that of knowing that we do your will. Amen.

St Ignatius Loyola (1491-1556)

Prayer to St Anthony for things that are lost

O great St Anthony, who has received from God a special power to recover lost things, help me that I may find that which I am now seeking.

An Old French Prayer for Friends

Blessed Mother of those whose names you can read in my heart, watch over them with every care. Make their way easy and their labours fruitful. Dry their tears if they weep; sanctify their joys; raise their courage if they weaken; restore their hope if they lose heart, their health if they be ill, truth if they err, and repentance if they fall. Amen.

Oblatio Sui
(*Prayer of Self Dedication to Jesus Christ used by St Ignatius of Loyola*)

Súscipe, Dómine, univérsam mean libertátem. Accipe memóriam, intelléctum atque voluntatem omnem. Quidquid hábeo vel possídeo, mihi largítus es: id tibi totum restítuo, ac tuae prorsus voluntáti trado gubernándum. Amórem tui solum cum grátia tua mihi dones, et dives sum satis, nec áliud quidquam ultra posco.

Receive, O Lord, all my liberty. Take my memory, my understanding, and my entire will. Whatsoever I have or hold, you have given me; I give it all back to you and surrender it wholly to be governed by your will. Give me only your love and your grace, and I am rich enough and ask for nothing more.

Prayer of Blessed Teresa of Calcutta

The fruit of Silence is Prayer.
The fruit of Prayer is Faith.
The fruit of Faith is Love.
The fruit of Love is Service.

Founder of the Missionaries of Charity (1910-1997)

Prayer of Daily Service

Make us worthy, Lord, to serve our fellow men throughout the world who live and die in poverty and hunger. Give them through our hands this day their daily bread, and by our understanding love, give peace and joy. Make us, Lord, worthy to serve our brothers and sisters who are scattered all over the world, who live and die alone and poor. Give them today, using our hands, their daily bread. And, using our love, give them peace and happiness.
Amen.

Prayer of St Teresa of Avila

My God, dispose of me, and of all that belongs to me, according to your good pleasure.
Amen.

Prayer to the Sacred Heart of Jesus

Most sacred, most loving Heart of Jesus, you are concealed in the Holy Eucharist, and you bear for us still. Now, as then, you say: "With desire I have desired." I worship you with all my best love and awe, with fervent affection, with my most subdued, most resolved will. For a while you take up your abode within me. O make my heart beat with your Heart! Purify it of all that is earthly, all that is proud and sensual, of all perversity, of all disorder. So fill it with you, that neither the events of the day, nor the circumstance of the time, may have the power to ruffle it; but that in your love and your fear, it may have peace. Amen.

John Henry Cardinal Newman (1801-1890)

Evening Prayer of St Augustine

Watch, Lord, with those who wake or weep tonight. Give the angels and saints charge over those who sleep. O Lord Jesus Christ, tend your sick ones, rest your weary ones, bless your dying ones, soothe the suffering ones, pity all the afflicted ones, shield the joyful ones, and all for your love's sake.
Amen.

⁓ Preparing for Confession ⁓

De Profundis (*Ps 130*)

Out of the depths I cry to you, O Lord,
Lord, hear my voice!
O let your ears be attentive
to the voice of my pleading.
If you, O Lord, should mark our guilt,
Lord, who would survive?
But with you is found forgiveness;
for this we revere you.
My soul is waiting for the Lord,
I count on his word.
My soul is longing for the Lord,
more than watchmen for daybreak.
(Let the watchman count on daybreak
and Israel on the Lord.)
Because with the Lord there is mercy
and fullness of redemption,
Israel indeed he will redeem from all its iniquity.
Glory be to the Father, and to the Son,
and to the Holy Spirit;
as it was in the beginning,
is now, and ever shall be,
world without end. Amen.

Act of Contrition

My God, I am sorry for my sins with all my heart.
In choosing to do wrong
and failing to do good,
I have sinned against you
whom I should love above all things.
I firmly intend,
with your help,
to do penance,
to sin no more, and to avoid whatever leads me to sin.
Our Saviour Jesus Christ suffered and died for us.
In his name, my God, have mercy.
Amen.

*This prayer is taken from the revised
Rite of Penance, 1974*

Traditional

O my God,
I am heartily sorry for having offended thee,
and I detest all my sins,
because I dread the loss of heaven,
and the pains of hell;
but most of all because
they offend thee, my God,
Who are all good and

deserving of all my love.
I firmly resolve, with the help of thy grace,
to sin no more and avoid the near occasions of sin.
Amen.

Shorter Act of Contrition suitable for children

Oh my God, because you are so good, I am truly sorry that I have sinned against you, and by the help of your grace I will not sin again.

Confíteor	I Confess
Confíteor Deo omnipoténti et vobis, fratres,	I confess to almighty God and to you, my brothers and sisters,
quia peccávi nimis cogitatióne, verbo, ópere et omissióne:	that I have greatly sinned in my thoughts and in my words, in what I have done and in what I have failed to do,
et, percutientes sibi pectus, dicunt:	*And, striking their breast, they say:*
mea culpa,	through my fault,
mea culpa,	through my fault,
mea máxima culpa.	through my most grievous fault;

Deinde prosequuntur:	*Then they continue*:
Ideo precor beátam	therefore I ask blessed
Maríam semper Vírginem,	Mary ever Virgin,
omnes Angelos et Sanctos,	all the Angels and Saints,
et vos, fratres,	and you, my brothers
	and sisters,
oráre pro me	to pray for me to the
ad Dóminum Deum	Lord our God.
nostrum.	

Act of Contrition

O God, loose, remit, and forgive my sins against you,
whether in word, in deed, or in thought;
and whether they are willingly or unwillingly,
knowingly or unknowingly committed, forgive them all.
For you are good and you love all human beings.
And through the prayers of your most holy Mother,
or your heavenly servants and holy spirits,
and all the saints who have found favour with you,
enable me to receive without condemnation your holy
Body and your Precious Blood.
Let my soul and body be thus healed and my evil
imaginings be driven away, for yours is the kingdom,
the power, and the glory:
Father, Son, and Holy Spirit, now and forever.
Amen.

St John Chrysostom (adapted)

Prayer of Firm Purpose of Amendment

O Lord, I place myself in your hands and dedicate myself to you. I pledge myself to do your will in all things: to love the Lord God with all my heart, all my soul, all my strength. Not to kill. Not to steal. Not to covet. Not to bear false witness. To honour all persons. Not to do to another what I would not wish done to myself. To chastise the body. Not to seek after pleasures. To love fasting. To relieve the poor. To clothe the naked. To visit the sick. To bury the dead. To help in trouble. To console the sorrowing. To hold myself aloof from worldly ways. To prefer nothing to the love of Christ. Not to give way to anger. Not to foster a desire for revenge. Not to entertain deceit in the heart. Not to make a false peace. Not to forsake charity. Not to swear, lest I swear falsely. To speak the truth with heart and tongue. Not to return evil for evil. To do no injury: yes, even to bear patiently any injury done to me. To love my enemies. Not to curse those who curse me, but rather to bless them. To bear persecution for justice's sake. Not to be proud. Not to be given to intoxicating drink. Not to be an overeater. Not to be lazy. Not to be slothful. Not to be a murmurer. Not to be a detractor. To put my trust in God. To refer the good I see in myself to God. To refer any evil in myself to myself. To fear the day of judgement. To be in dread of hell. To desire eternal life with spiritual longing. To keep death before my eyes daily. To keep constant watch over my actions. To remember that God sees me everywhere. To call upon Christ for defence against evil thoughts that arise in my heart. To guard my tongue against wicked speech. To avoid much speaking. To avoid idle talk. To read only what is good to read. To look at only what is good to see. To pray often. To ask forgiveness daily for my sins, and to seek ways to amend my life. To obey my superiors in all things rightful. Not to desire to be thought holy, but to seek holiness. To fulfil the commandments of God by good works. To love chastity. To hate no one. Not to be jealous or envious of anyone. Not to love strife. Not to love pride. To honour the aged. To pray for my enemies. To make peace after a quarrel, before the setting of the sun. Never to despair of your mercy, O God of Mercy. Amen.

Prayer of St Benedict of Nursia (480-547)

Prayer for Divine Mercy

O Greatly Merciful God, Infinite Goodness, today all mankind calls out from the abyss of its misery to your mercy, to your compassion, O God; and it is with its mighty voice of misery that it cries out: Gracious God, do not reject the prayer of this earth's exiles! O

Lord, goodness beyond our understanding, who are acquainted with our misery through and through, and know that by our power we cannot ascend to you, we implore you, anticipate us with your grace and keep on increasing your mercy in us, that we may faithfully do your holy will all through our life and at death's hour. Let the omnipotence of your mercy shield us from the darts of our salvation's enemies, that we may with confidence, as your children, await your final coming - that day known to you alone. And we expect to obtain everything promised us by Jesus in spite of all our wretchedness. For Jesus is our Hope: through His merciful Heart as through an open gate we pass through to heaven.

From the Diary of St Maria Faustina of the Sisters of Our Lady of Mercy (1905-1938)

~ PREPARING FOR MASS ~ AND HOLY COMMUNION

Prayer of St Ambrose

Lord Jesus Christ,
I approach your banquet table in fear and trembling,
for I am a sinner and dare not rely on my own worth
but only on your goodness and mercy.
I am defiled by many sins in body and soul
and by my unguarded thoughts and words.
Gracious God of majesty and awe,
I seek your protection,
I look for your healing.
Poor troubled sinner that I am,
I appeal to you, the fountain of all mercy.
I cannot bear your judgement,
but I trust in your salvation.
Lord, I show my wounds to you
and uncover my shame before you.
I know my sins are many and great
and they fill me with fear,
but I hope in your mercies,
for they cannot be numbered.
Lord Jesus Christ, eternal king,
divine and human,

crucified for humanity,
look upon me with mercy and hear my prayer,
for I trust in you...
Have mercy on me,
full of sorrow and sin,
for the depth of your compassion never ends.
Praise to you, saving sacrifice,
offered on the wood of the cross for me and for all.
Praise to the noble and precious blood
flowing from the wounds of my crucified Lord
Jesus Christ and washing away the sins of the
whole world.
Remember, Lord, your creatures,
whom you have redeemed with your blood.
I repent of my sins
and I long to put right what I have done.
Merciful Lord, take away all my offences and sins;
purify me in body and soul,
and make me worthy to taste the holy of holies.
May your body and blood,
which I intend to receive, although I am unworthy,
be for me the remission of my sins,
the washing away of my guilt,
the end of my evil thoughts
and the rebirth of my better instincts.

May it spur me on to works pleasing to you and be profitable to my health in body and soul and a firm defence against the wiles of my enemies. Amen.

Preparation for Mass; attributed to St Ambrose
(c. 339-397), bishop of Milan

Prayer of St Augustine

Lord Jesus, let me know myself and know you,
And desire nothing, save only you.
Let me hate myself and love you.
Let me do everything for the sake of you.
Let me humble myself and exalt you.
Let me think of nothing except you.
Let me accept whatever happens as from you.
Let me banish self and follow you,
And ever desire to follow you.
Let me fly from myself and take refuge in you,
That I may deserve to be defended by you.
Let me fear for myself, let me fear you,
And let me be among those who are chosen by you.
Let me be willing to obey for the sake of you.
Let me cling to nothing, save only to you,
And let me be poor because of you.
Look upon me, that I may love you.
Call me, that I may see you,
And for ever enjoy you. Amen.

Prayer of St Thomas Aquinas

Almighty and ever-living God,
I approach the sacrament of your only-begotten Son,
our Lord Jesus Christ.
I come sick to the doctor of life,
unclean to the fountain of mercy,
blind to the radiance of eternal light,
poor and needy to the Lord of heaven and earth.
Lord in your great generosity,
heal my sickness, wash away my defilement,
enlighten my blindness, enrich my poverty,
and clothe my nakedness.
May I receive the bread of angels,
the King of kings and Lord of lords,
with humble reverence,
with purity and faith,
with the repentance and love
and the determined purpose
that will help to bring me to salvation.
May I receive the sacrament of the Lord's
body and blood
and its reality and power.
Kind God,
may I receive the body of your only begotten Son,
our Lord Jesus Christ,

born from the womb of the Virgin Mary,
and so be received into his mystical body
and numbered among his members.
Loving Father,
as on my earthly pilgrimage
I now receive your beloved Son
under the veil of a sacrament,
may I one day see him face to face in glory,
who lives and reigns with you forever. Amen.

Preparation for Mass;
attributed to St Thomas Aquinas (c. 1225-1274)

Adoro Te Devote

Adóro te devóte, latens Déitas, Quae sub his figúris vere látitas: Tibi se cor meum totum súbiicit, Quia te contémplans totum déficit.

Hidden here before me, Lord, I worship you, Hidden in these symbols, yet completely true. Lord, my soul surrenders, I longing to obey, And in contemplation wholly faints away.

Visus, tactus, gustus in te fállitur, Sed audítu solo tuto créditur.

Seeing, touching, tasting; these are all deceived;

Credo, quidquid dixit
Dei Fílius: Nic hoc verbo
Veritátis vérius.

Only through the hearing
can it be believed.
Nothing is more certain;
Christ has told me so;
What the Truth has
uttered, I believe
and know.

In cruce latébat sola
Déitas, At hic latet simul
et humánitas; Ambo
tamen credens atque
cónfitens, Peto quod
petívit latro paénitens.

Only God was hidden
when you came to die;
Human nature also here
escapes the eye. Both are
my profession, both are
my belief; Bring me to
your kingdom like the
dying thief.

Plagas, sicut Thomas, non
intúeor; Deum tamen
meum te confíteor.
Fac me tibi semper magis
crédere, In te spem
habére, te dilígere.

I am not like Thomas,
who could see and touch;
Though your wounds are
hidden, I believe as much.
Let me say so boldly,
meaning what I say.
Loving you and trusting,
now and every day.

O memoriále mortis
Dómini! Panis vivus,
vitam praestans hómini!
Praesta meae menti de te
vívere. Et te illi semper
dulce sápere.

Record of the Passion
when the Lamb was slain,
Living bread that brings
us back to life again; Feed
me with your presence,
make me live on you; Let
that lovely fragrance fill
me through and through.

Pie pellicáne, Iesu
Dómine, Me immúndum
munda tuo sánguine.
Cuius una stilla salvum
fácere Totum mundum
quit ab omni scélere.

Once a nesting pelican
gashed herself to blood
For the preservation of
her starving brood; Now
heal me with your blood,
take away my guilt; All the
world is ransomed if one
drop is spilt.

Iesu, quem velátum nunc
aspício, Oro fiat illud
quod tam sítio; Ut te
reveláta cernens fácie,
Visu sim beátus tuae
glóriae.

Jesus, for the present seen
as through a mask, Give
me what I thirst for, give
me what I ask; Let me
see your glory in a blaze
of light, And instead of
blindness give me, Lord,

Amen.

my sight. Amen.

Attributed to St Thomas Aquinas (c. 1225-1274)

The Prayer of Humble Access

We do not presume to come to this your table,
O merciful Lord, trusting in our own
righteousness,
but in your many and great mercies.
We are not worthy even to gather up
the crumbs under your table.

But you are the same God whose property
is always to have mercy:
grant us, therefore, gracious Lord,
so to eat the flesh of your dear Son Jesus Christ,
and to drink his blood,
that our sinful bodies may be made clean by his body,
and our souls washed through his most precious blood,
and that we may evermore dwell in him and he in us.

The Book of Common Prayer,
based on a prayer of St Ambrose

Prayer of Thomas à Kempis

Lord Jesus Christ,
to whom belongs all that is in heaven and earth,
I desire to consecrate myself wholly to you and be yours
for evermore.
This day I offer myself to you in singleness of heart,

to serve and obey you always,
and I offer you without ceasing a sacrifice of praise
and thanksgiving.
Receive me, O my Saviour,
in union with the holy oblation of your precious blood
which I offer to you this day,
in the presence of angels,
that this sacrifice may avail unto my salvation and that of
the whole world.

Prayer of St Thomas More

Give me, good Lord, a full faith, and fervent charity,
a love of you, good Lord,
incomparable above the love of myself;
and that I love nothing to your displeasure,
but everything in order to serve you.
Take from me, good Lord,
this lukewarm fashion, or rather,
this cold manner of meditation,
and this dullness in praying to you.
Give me warmth, delight, and life in thinking about you.
And give me your grace to long for your holy sacraments
and specially to rejoice in the presence of your blessed
body, my sweet Saviour Jesus Christ,
in the holy sacrament of the altar, and duly to thank you
for your graciousness in giving yourself to me.

Anima Christi

Anima Christi,
sanctífica me.
Corpus Christi, salva me.
Sanguis Christi, inébria
me. Aqua láteris Christi,
lava me. Pássio Christi,
confórta me.

O bone Iesu, exáudi me.
Intra tua vúlnera
abscónde me.

Ne permíttas me separári
a te. Ab hoste malígno
defénde me.

In hora mortis meae voca
me. Et iube me venire
ad te, ut cum Sanctis
tuis laudem te in sáecula
saeculórum.
Amen.

Soul of Christ, sanctify
me. Body of Christ,
heal me. Blood of Christ,
drench me. Water from
the side of Christ, wash
me. Passion of Christ,
strengthen me.

Good Jesus, hear me.
In your wounds shelter
me.

From turning away keep
me. From the evil one
protect me.

At the hour of my
death call me. Into your
presence lead me, to
praise you with all your
saints forever and ever.
Amen.

*Thanksgiving after Mass; early fourteenth century,
familiar in English as the hymn 'Soul of my Saviour'*

Prayer for protection after Mass

St Michael the Archangel, defend us in the day of battle.
Be our safeguard against the wickedness and snares of
the devil,
may God rebuke him, we humbly pray.
And do thou, O Prince of the heavenly hosts,
by the power of God,
cast down into hell Satan, and all those evil spirits
who wander through the world for the ruin of souls.
Amen.

Prayer of Thanksgiving after Mass

Lord, Father, all-powerful and ever-living God.
I thank you,
for even though I am a sinner
and your unprofitable servant,
you have fed me with the precious body
and blood of your Son,
our Lord Jesus Christ, not because of my worth
but out of your kindness and your mercy.
I pray that this Holy Communion
may not bring me condemnation and punishment
but forgiveness and salvation.
May it be a helmet of faith
and a shield of good will.

May it purify me from evil ways
and put an end to my evil passions.
May it bring me charity and patience,
humility and obedience,
and growth in the power to do good.
May it be my strong defence
against all my enemies, visible and invisible,
and the perfect calming of all my evil impulses,
bodily and spiritual.
May it unite me more closely to you,
the one true God,
and lead me safely through death
to everlasting happiness with you.
And I pray that you will lead me, a sinner,
to the banquet where you,
with your Son and the Holy Spirit
are true and perfect light,
total fulfilment, everlasting joy, gladness without end,
and perfect happiness to your saints.
Grant this through Christ our Lord. Amen.

Tantum Ergo

Therefore we, before him bending,
This great Sacrament revere;
Types and shadows have their ending
for the newer rite is here;

Faith, our outward sense befriending,
Makes the inward vision clear.

Glory let us give, and blessing
To the Father and the Son;
Honour, might, and praise addressing,
While eternal ages run;
Ever to his love confessing,
Who, from both, with both is one. Amen.

*Last two verses of a hymn written about 1264
by St Thomas Aquinas (c. 1225-1274)*

Prayer of Self-Dedication to Jesus Christ

Lord Jesus Christ,
take my freedom,
my memory, my understanding and my will.
All that I have and cherish,
you have given me.
I surrender it all to be guided by your will.
Your grace and your love are wealth enough for me.
Give me these, Lord Jesus,
and I ask for nothing more.

*Thanksgiving after Mass attributed
to St Ignatius Loyola (c. 1491-1556)*

St Teresa's Bookmark

Let nothing disturb you,
Nothing frighten you.
All things are passing,
God never changes.
Patient endurance attains all things.
Whom God possesses in nothing is wanting.
Alone God suffices.

St Teresa of Avila (1515-1582)

Act of Petition

Give me yourself,
O my God, give yourself to me.
Behold I love you,
and if my love is too weak a thing,
grant me to love you more strongly.
I cannot measure my love to know how much it falls
short of being sufficient,
but let my soul hasten to your embrace
and never be turned away until it is hidden
in the secret shelter of your presence.
This only do I know,
that it is not good for me when you are not with me,
when you are only outside me.
I want you in my very self.

All the plenty in the world
which is not my God is utter want.

St Augustine of Hippo

Prayer before a crucifix

G ood and gentle Jesus,
I kneel before you.
I see and ponder your five wounds.
My eyes behold what David prophesied about you;

"They have pierced my hands and feet;
they have counted all my bones."
Engrave on me this image of yourself.
Fulfill the yearnings of my heart;
give me faith, hope and love,
repentance for my sins and true conversion of life.
Amen.

*This prayer of thanksgiving after Mass
is as given in the Roman Missal since 1570*

~ Prayers to Our Lady ~

Hail Mary

The first three lines (the first two in some sources) are the Salutation of the Archangel Gabriel to the future mother of Jesus. The third line is echoed by Elizabeth her cousin who adds also the fourth line. The addition of the word 'Jesus' is attributed to Pope Urban IV, while the concluding petition is the prayer of the Church and reached its present form in 1514.

Ave María,
gratia plena,
Dóminus tecum;
Benedícta tu in
muliéribus,
et benedíctus fructus
ventris tui, Iesus.

Sancta Maria,
Mater Dei,
ora pro nobis
peccatoribus,
nunc et in hora
mortis nostrae. Amen.

Hail, Mary,
full of grace,
the Lord is with thee;
blessed art thou
among women,
and blessed is the fruit
of thy womb, Jesus.

Holy Mary,
Mother of
God, pray for
us sinners,
now, and at the hour of
our death. Amen.

How to Say the Rosary

"The Rosary is a gospel prayer. The orderly and gradual unfolding of the Rosary reflects the very way in which the Word of God, mercifully entering into human affairs, brought about redemption." (Pope Paul VI, *Marialis Cultus* (1974, n. 44). St John Paul II added the Luminous Mysteries, or Mysteries of Light, during his pontificate in order that we could meditate not only on the beginning and end of our Saviour's life, but also on the great signs he performed while here on earth.

If you have a set of rosary beads, first kiss the crucifix, then make the sign of the cross holding the Rosary in your right hand and say:

In the name of the Father, and of the Son, and of the Holy Spirit. Amen.

Then on the first bead above the crucifix say:

The Apostles' Creed

Credo in Deum, Patrem omnipoténtem, Creatórem caeli et terrae. Et in Iesum Christum, Fílium eius únicum,

I believe in God, the Father almighty, Creator of heaven and earth, and in Jesus Christ, his only Son, our Lord, who

Dóminum nostrum: qui concéptus est de Spíritu Sancto, natus ex María Vírgine, passus sub Póntio Piláto, crucifíxus, mórtuus, et sepúltus; descéndit ad inferos; tértia die resurréxit a mórtuis; ascéndit ad caelos; sedet ad déxteram Dei Patris omnipoténtis; inde ventúrus est iudicáre vivos et mórtuos. Credo in Spíritum Sanctum, sanctam Ecclésiam Cathólicam, Sanctórum communiónem, remissiónem peccatórum, carnis resurrectiónem, vitam aetérnam. Amen.

was conceived by the Holy Spirit, born of the Virgin Mary, suffered under Pontius Pilate, was crucified, died and was buried; he descended into hell; on the third day he rose again from the dead; he ascended into heaven, and is seated at the right hand of God the Father almighty; from there he will come to judge the living and the dead. I believe in the Holy Spirit, the holy Catholic Church, the communion of saints, the forgiveness of sins, the resurrection of the body, and life everlasting. Amen.

Then on each of the three following beads say the:

Hail Mary (see p. 63).

Traditionally these three Hail Marys are said for the intentions of the Holy Father.

On the first bead in the main part of the Rosary say:
The Lord's Prayer (see p. 16)

This is followed by ten Hail Marys on the next ten beads. The decade is concluded with a:
Glory be (see p. 17)

We can add the prayer from the vision at Fatima:

O my Jesus, forgive us our sins, save us from the fires of hell, and lead all souls to heaven, especially those in most need of Your Mercy.

While saying these prayers we also meditate on the events of the life of Christ and of his mother. These are called the mysteries of the Rosary.

A complete Rosary consists of twenty decades, but it is usual to say five at a time.

The Mysteries of the Rosary

The Joyful Mysteries are said on Mondays and Saturdays.
The Mysteries of Light on Thursdays.
The Sorrowful on Tuesdays and Fridays.
The Glorious on Wednesdays and Sundays.

The twenty mysteries are:

The Five Joyful Mysteries

1. The Annunciation
2. The Visitation
3. The Nativity
4. The Presentation in the Temple
5. The Finding of the Child Jesus in the Temple

The Five Mysteries of Light

1. The Baptism in the Jordan
2. The Wedding at Cana
3. The Proclamation of the Kingdom of God
4. The Transfiguration
5. The Institution of the Eucharist

The Five Sorrowful Mysteries

1. The Prayer and Agony in the Garden
2. The Scourging at the Pillar
3. The Crowning with Thorns
4. The Carrying of the Cross
5. The Crucifixion and Death of Our Lord

The Five Glorious Mysteries

1. The Resurrection
2. The Ascension of Christ into Heaven
3. The Descent of the Holy Spirit on the Apostles
4. The Assumption of Our Lady into Heaven
5. The Coronation of the Blessed Virgin Mary in Heaven and the Glory of all the Saints

After the last mystery we say the:
Salve Regina (Hail Holy Queen)

Salve, Regína, mater misericórdiae; vita, dulcédo, et spes nostra, salve. Ad te clamámus, éxsules fílii Evae.
Ad te suspirámus, geméntes et flentes in hac lacrimárum valle.
Eia ergo, advocáta nostra, illos tuos misericórdes óculos ad nos converte.
Et Iesum, benedíctum fructum ventris tui, nobis post hoc exsílium osténde.

O clemens, O pia,
O dulcis Virgo María.

V. Ora pro nobis sancta Dei Génetrix.

R. Ut digni efficiamur promissiónibus Christi.

Hail, Holy Queen, Mother of Mercy; hail, our life, our sweetness and our hope. To thee do we cry, poor banished children of Eve; to thee do we send up our sighs, mourning and weeping in this valley of tears. Turn then, most gracious advocate, thine eyes of mercy towards us; and after this our exile, show unto us the blessed fruit of thy womb Jesus.

O clement, O loving, O sweet Virgin Mary.

V. Pray for us O Holy Mother of God.

R. That we may be made worthy of the promises of Christ.

Orémus

Déus, cújus Unigénitus per vítam, mórtem et resurrectiónem súam nóbis salútis ætérnæ præmia comparávit: concéde, quæsumus: ut hæc mystéria sacratíssimo beátæ Maríæ Vírginis Rosário recoléntes, et imitémur quod cóntinent, et quod promíttunt, assequámur. Per eúndem Chrístum Dóminum nóstrum.

R. Amen.

Let us pray

O God, whose only begotten Son, by his life, death and resurrection, has purchased for us the rewards of eternal life; grant we beseech thee, that meditating on these mysteries of the most holy Rosary of the Blessed Virgin Mary, we may both imitate what they contain and obtain what they promise, through the same Christ Our Lord.

R. Amen.

Attributed to several sources; probable author Herman the Lame (1013-1054), a monk of Reichenau

The Angelus

The custom of saying the Angelus at 6 a.m., noon and 6 p.m. goes back to the thirteenth century.

V. Angelus Dómini, nuntiávit Maríæ,

V. The angel of the Lord declared unto Mary,

R. Et concépit de Spíritu Sancto.

Ave María...

V. Ecce ancilla Domini.

R. Fiat mihi secúndum verbum tuum.

Ave María...

V. Et Verbum caro factum est,

R. Et habitávit in nobis

Ave Maria...

V. Ora pro nobis, sancta Dei Génetrix,

R. Ut digni efficiámur promissiónibus Christi.

R. And she conceived of the Holy Spirit.

Hail Mary...

V. Behold the handmaid of the Lord.

R. Be it done to me according to thy word.

Hail Mary...

V. And the word was made flesh,

R. And dwelt among us.

Hail Mary...

V. Pray for us O holy Mother of God,

R. That we may be made worthy of the promises of Christ.

Orémus

Grátiam tuam, quaésumus, Dómine, méntibus nostris infúnde; ut qui, ángelo nuntiánte, Christi Fílii tui incarnatiónem cognóvimus, per

Let us pray

Pour forth, we beseech thee O Lord, thy grace into our hearts that we to whom the incarnation of Christ, thy Son, was made known by the message of an angel, may by his

passiónem eius et crucem ✛, ad resurrectiónis glóriam perducámur. Per eúndem Christum Dóminum nostrum.
R. Amen.

passion and cross be brought to the glory of his resurrection through the same Christ, Our Lord.
R. Amen.

Regina Caeli (by Gregory V)

A twelfth century Evening Prayer antiphon for the Easter Season. Since the thirteenth century, it has been used as the seasonal antiphon in honour of the Blessed Virgin after Night Prayer. Since 1743 it has replaced the Angelus in the Easter Season.

Regína caeli, laetáre.
Allelúia.
Quia quem meruísti portáre.
Allelúia.
Resurréxit, sicut dixit.
Allelúia.
Ora pro nobis, Deum.
Allelúia.
Gaude et laetáre,
Virgo María,
Allelúia.

Queen of heaven, rejoice.
Alleluia.
For he whom you did merit to bear.
Alleluia.
Has risen as he said.
Alleluia.
Pray for us to God.
Alleluia.
Rejoice and be glad, O Virgin Mary.
Alleluia.

Quia surréxit
Dominus vere.
Allelúia.

Orémus

Deus, qui per
resurrectiónem
Fílii tui, Dómini nostri
Iesu Christi, mundum
laetificáre dignátus es:
praesta, quáesumus;
ut, per eius Genitrícem
Vírginem Maríam,
pérpetuae capiámus
gáudia vitae. Per eúndem
Christum Dóminum
nostrum.
R. Amen.

For the Lord has
truly risen.
Alleluia.

Let us pray

O God, who gave joy to
the world through the
resurrection of your Son
our Lord Jesus Christ,
grant, we beseech
you, that through the
intercession of the Virgin
Mary, his Mother, we
may obtain the joys of
everlasting life, through
Christ our Lord.
R. Amen.

A Child's Prayer to Mary

Mary, mother whom we bless,
full of grace and tenderness,
defend me from the devil's power
and greet me in my dying hour.

From the hymn Memento Rerum Conditur

Memorare

Memoráre, o piíssima Virgo María, non esse audítum a saéculo, quemquam ad tua curréntem praesídia, tua implorántem auxília, tua peténtem suffrágia esse derelíctum.

Ego tali animátus confidéntia ad te, Virgo Vírginum, Mater, curro; ad te vénio; coram te gemens peccátor assísto.

Noli, Mater Verbi, verba mea despícere, sed audi propitia et exáudi. Amen.

Remember, O most loving Virgin Mary, that never was it known that anyone who fled to thy protection, implored thy help, or sought thy intercession, was left unaided.

Inspired by this confidence I fly unto thee, O Virgin of virgins, my Mother.
To thee do I come, before thee I stand, sinful and sorrowful.

O Mother of the Word Incarnate, despise not my petitions, but in thy mercy hear and answer me Amen.

Ascribed to St Bernard (1090-1153)

Prayer for England

In the Middle Ages, England was known as Our Lady's Dowry, because it is said that there were more churches dedicated to Mary than to any other saint.

This prayer, in its original form written by Cardinal Merry del Val, has traditionally been said at Benediction. It is a prayer for the unity of the Church in England.

O Blessed Virgin Mary, Mother of God, and our most gentle queen and mother, look down in mercy upon England, your dowry, and upon us all who greatly hope and trust in you. By you it was that Jesus, our Saviour and our hope, was given to the world; and he has given you to us that we may hope still more.

Plead for us your children, whom you received and accepted at the foot of the cross, O Mother of sorrows. Pray for our separated brethren, that in the one true fold of Christ, we may all be united under the care of Pope N., the chief shepherd of Christ's flock. Pray for us all, dear mother, that by faith, and fruitful in good works, we may all deserve to see and praise God, together with you in our heavenly home.

We Fly to Thy Protection

Sub Tuum Praesidium

Sub tuum praesidium confugimus, Sancta Dei Genetrix, nostras deprecationes ne despicias in necessitatibus nostris, sed a periculis cunctis libera nos semper, Virgo gloriosa et benedicta.
Amen.

We fly to thy protection, O holy Mother of God, despise not our petitions in our necessities, but deliver us always from all dangers, O glorious and blessed Virgin.

Amen.

The Church's Oldest Prayer to Our Lady

Translation of the Greek from which the prayer Sub Tuum is derived.

O Mother of God, we take refuge in your loving care. Let not our plea to you pass unheeded in the trials that beset us, but deliver us from danger, for you alone are truly pure, you alone are truly blessed.

Tota Pulchra Es

Tota pulchra es, Maria, et macula originalis non est in te.

You are all beautiful, Mary, and there is no original stain in you.

Totus Tuus

Totus tuus ego sum, et omnia mea tua sunt, O Virgo, super omnia benedicta.

I am all yours, and all that is mine is yours, O Virgin, blessed above all.

St Louis-Marie Grignon de Montfort (1673-1716)

Maria, Mater Gratiae

Maria, Mater gratiae, Mater misericordiae, tu me ab hoste protege et mortis hora suscipe.

Mary, Mother of grace, Mother of mercy, protect me from the enemy and receive me at the hour of death.

Sancta Maria, Succurre Miseris

Sancta Maria, succurre miseris, iuva pusillanimes, refove flebiles, ora pro populo, interveni pro clero, intercede pro devoto femineo sexu: sentiant omnes tuum iuvamen, quiccumque celebrant tuam sanctam commemorationem.

Holy Mary, hasten to the aid of the afflicted, support the faint-hearted, comfort the sorrowful, pray for your people, intercede on behalf of the clergy, intercede for devout women; may all who celebrate your holy memory come to know your assistance.

Prayer for Mary's guidance

O Mary, child of the Father's loving heart,
Blest spouse of the Holy Spirit
and Mother of the world's Redeemer,
Pray for us who stumble in the darkness of this world
That we may be guided by your gentle hand
into the light of heaven.

Prayers of consecration to Our Lady

Immaculate Heart of Mary, I give you my heart.
I want to love you and I want to love Jesus,
the Father, the Holy Spirit,
and this world through your holy heart.
My dear Mother, I place myself in your heart,
I know you will care for me in all my needs.
I give myself to you, Mary, my Mother;
teach me to love you more.

O Mary, Virgin most powerful and Mother of mercy,
Queen of heaven and refuge of sinners,
we consecrate ourselves to your Immaculate Heart.

We consecrate to you our very being and our whole life;
all that we have, all that we love, all that we are.

To you we give our bodies, our hearts and our souls;
to you we give our homes, our families, our country.

We desire that all that is in us and around us may
   belong to you,
and may share in the benefits of your motherly
   benediction.

And that this act of consecration may be truly efficacious
and lasting,
we renew this day at your feet the promises of our
baptism and our first Holy Communion.

We pledge ourselves to profess courageously and at all
   times the truths of our holy Faith,
and to live as befits Catholics who are duly submissive
   to all the directions
of the Pope and the bishops in communion with him.
Amen.

~ In Sickness and Death ~

Prayer for a Happy Death

Father, you made us in your own image and your Son accepted death for our salvation.
Help us to keep watch in prayer at all times.
May we be free from sin when we leave this world and rejoice in peace with you for ever.

From the Roman Missal

Prayer for the Sick

Father, your Son accepted our sufferings to teach us the virtue of patience in human illness.
Hear the prayers we offer for our sick brothers and sisters.
May all who suffer pain, illness or disease realise that they are chosen to be saints and know that they are joined to Christ in his suffering for the salvation of the world.

From the Roman Missal

Prayer for the Dying

God of power and mercy, you have made death itself the gateway to eternal life.
Look with love on our dying brother (sister) and make him (her) one with your Son in his suffering and death, that, sealed with the blood of Christ, he (she) may come before you free from sin.

From the Roman Missal

Prayer for the Dead

This is the traditional Introit from the Mass for the Dead

Eternal rest grant unto them, O Lord
and let perpetual light shine upon them.

Prayer Immediately after Death

Immediately after death has occurred, all may kneel while one of those present leads the following prayer:

Saints of God, come to his/her aid!
Come to meet him/her, angels of the Lord!

R. Receive him/her, angels of the Lord!
May Christ, who called you, take you to himself;
may angels lead you to Abraham's side. **R.**

Give him/her eternal rest, O Lord, and may your light
shine on him/her for ever. **R.**

The following prayer is added:
Let us pray.
All powerful and merciful God, we commend to you N.,
your servant. In your mercy and love,
blot out the sins he/she has committed through human
weakness.
In this world he/she died: let him/her live with you for
ever.
We ask this through Christ our Lord. **R.** Amen.

⌁ Exposition and Benediction ⌁

Rite of Exposition and Benediction

Toward the beginning of the thirteenth century, great emphasis was being placed on the truth of the Real Presence of Christ in the Blessed Sacrament. Although Catholics had always believed that Jesus is actually present in the Eucharist, the fact was now being stressed to counteract some false ideas that were prevalent at the time. To correct mistaken notions and even superstition in regard to the doctrine, the Church fostered a renewal in the faith and devotion toward the Real Presence. In 1246, the feast of Corpus Christi, honouring the Body of Our Lord, was established. Also in this period, St Thomas Aquinas, the 'Angelic Doctor', composed his beautiful hymns praising the Holy Eucharist.

(Anthony Teolis, 'Mary at Benediction',
Homiletic and Pastoral Review, vol. XCVII, no. 2, p. 54)

Exposition

After the people have assembled, a song may be sung while the minister comes to the altar. If the holy Eucharist is not reserved at the altar where the exposition is to take place, the minister puts on a humeral veil and brings the sacrament from the place of reservation; he is accompanied by servers or by the faithful with lighted candles. The ciborium or monstrance should be placed upon the table of the altar, which is covered with a cloth. After exposition, if the monstrance is used, the minister incenses the sacrament. If the adoration is to be lengthy, he may then withdraw.

Adoration

During the exposition there should be prayers, songs and readings to direct the attention of the faithful to the worship of Christ the Lord.

To encourage a prayerful spirit, there should be readings from Scripture with a homily or brief exhortation to develop a better understanding of the Eucharistic mystery. It is desirable also for the people to respond to the word of God by singing and to spend some periods of time in religious silence. During a longer period of adoration, such as a Holy Hour, the Rosary may be said.

Part of the Liturgy of the Hours, especially the principal hours, may be celebrated before the Blessed Sacrament when there is a lengthy period of exposition. This liturgy extends the praise and thanksgiving offered to God in the Eucharistic celebration to the several hours of the day; it directs the prayers of the Church to Christ and through him to the Father in the name of the whole world. One of the following hymns may be sung:

O salutáris Hóstia
Quae caeli pandis
óstium.

Bella premunt hostília;
Da robur fer auxílium.

Uni trinóque Dómino
Sit sempitérna glória:

Qui vitam sine término,
Nobis donet in pátria.

Amen.

O Saving Victim
opening wide the
gates of heav'n to man
below!

Our foes press on from
every side; thine aid
supply, thy strength
bestow.

To thy great name be
endless praise Immortal
Godhead, One in Three;

Oh, grant us endless
length of days, in our true
native land with thee.

Amen.

or: Adoro Te Devote (p. 52)

Benediction
Eucharistic hymn and incensation

Toward the end, the priest or deacon goes to the altar, genuflects and kneels. As a hymn or other Eucharistic song is sung, the minister, while kneeling, incenses the sacrament, if the exposition has taken place with the monstrance. A hymn such as the following may be sung:

Tantum ergo
   Sacraméntum
Venerémur cérnui:
Et antíquum documéntum
Novo cedat rítui:
Praestet fides
suppleméntum
Sénsuum deféctui.

Therefore we, before
   him bending,
This great Sacrament
revere; Types and shadows
have their ending for
the newer rite is here;
Faith, our outward sense
befriending, Makes the
inward vision clear.

Genitóri, Genitóque
Laus et jubilátio.
Salus, honor, virtus
quoque Sit et benedíctio;
Procedénti ab utróque;
Compar sit laudátio.

Glory let us give, and
blessing to the Father and
the Son; Honour, might
and praise addressing,
While eternal ages run;
Ever to his love
confessing,
Who, from both, with
both is one.

Amen.

Amen.

V. Panem de caelo
praestítisti eis
(T.P. Allelúia).

R. Omne delectaméntum
in se habéntem
(T.P. Alleluia).

Orémus

Deus, qui nobis sub sacraménto mirábili, passiónis tuae memoriam reliquísti: tríbue, quaésumus, ita nos córporis et Sánguinis tui sacra mystéria venerári, ut redemptiónis tuae fructum in nobis iúgiter sentiámus: Qui vivis et regnas saécula saeculórum.

R. Amen.

Let us Pray

Lord Jesus Christ, you gave us the Eucharist as the memorial of your suffering and death. May our worship of this sacrament of your body and blood help us to experience the salvation you won for us and the peace of the kingdom where you live with the Father and the Holy Spirit, one God, for ever and ever.

R. Amen.

V. You have given them bread from heaven.
   (Easter time: Alleluia.)
R. Having all sweetness within it.
   (Easter Time: Alleluia.)

Let us pray. Lord Jesus Christ, you gave us the Eucharist as the memorial of your

Then the priest or deacon makes the sign of the cross over the people with the monstrance or ciborium, in silence.

The Divine Praises

Blessed be God.
Blessed be his holy Name.
Blessed be Jesus Christ, true God and true Man.
Blessed be the name of Jesus.
Blessed be his most Sacred Heart.
Blessed be his most Precious Blood.
Blessed be Jesus in the most holy Sacrament of the Altar.
Blessed be the Holy Spirit, the Paraclete.
Blessed be the great Mother of God, Mary, most holy.
Blessed be her holy and Immaculate Conception.
Blessed be her glorious Assumption.
Blessed be the name of Mary, Virgin and Mother.
Blessed be St Joseph, her spouse most chaste.
Blessed be God in his Angels and in his Saints.

~Evening Prayer~

An order for Evening Prayer

V.   O God, come to our aid.
R.   O Lord, make haste to help us.

Glory be to the Father, and to the Son, and to the Holy Spirit, as it was in the beginning, is now and ever shall be, world without end. Amen. (Alleluia.)

A suitable hymn such as one of the following is said:

O Trinity of blessed light,
O Unity of princely might,
The fiery sun now goes his way;
Shed thou within our hearts thy ray.

To thee our morning song of praise,
To thee our evening prayer we raise;
Thy glory suppliant we adore
For ever and for evermore.

All laud to God the Father be;
All praise, eternal Son, to thee;
All glory, as is ever meet,
To God the Holy Paraclete. Amen.

Before we end our day, O Lord,
we make this prayer to you:
That you continue in your love
to guard your people here.

Give us this night untroubled rest
and build our strength anew:
Your splendour driving far away
all darkness of the foe.

Our heart's desire to love you, Lord,
watch over while we sleep,
That when the new day dawns on high
we may your praises sing.

All glory be to you, O Christ,
who saved mankind from death -
To share with you the Father's love
and in the Spirit live.

Holy God, we praise thy Name;
Lord of all, we bow before thee!
All on earth thy sceptre claim,
All in heaven above adore thee;
Infinite thy vast domain,
Everlasting is thy reign.

Hark! the loud celestial hymn
Angel choirs above are raising,
Cherubim and seraphim,
In unceasing chorus praising;
Fill the heavens with sweet accord:
Holy, holy, holy, Lord.

Holy Father, Holy Son,
Holy Spirit, Three we name thee;
While in essence only One,
Undivided God we claim thee;
And adoring bend the knee,
While we own the mystery.

Spare thy people, Lord, we pray,
By a thousand snares surrounded:
Keep us without sin today,
Never let us be confounded.
Lo, I put my trust in thee;
Never, Lord, abandon me.

Praise to the Holiest in the height,
And in the depth be praise;
In all his words most wonderful,
Most sure in all his ways.

O loving wisdom of our God!
When all was sin and shame,
A second Adam to the fight
And to the rescue came.

O wisest love! that flesh and blood,
Which did in Adam fail,
Should strive afresh against the foe,
Should strive and should prevail.

And that a higher gift than grace
Should flesh and blood refine,
God's Presence and his very Self,
And Essence all divine.

O generous love! that he, who smote,
In Man for man the foe,
The double agony in Man
For man should undergo.

And in the garden secretly,
And on the cross on high,
Should teach his brethren, and inspire
To suffer and to die.

Praise to the Holiest in the height,
And in the depth be praise;
In all his words most wonderful,
Most sure in all his ways.

~

One or more of the following psalms can be said:

Psalm 110

The Lord's revelation to my Master;
"Sit on my right;
your foes I will put beneath your feet".

The Lord will wield from Sion
your sceptre of power;
rule in the midst of all your foes.

A prince from the day of your birth
on the holy mountains;
from the womb before the dawn I begot you.

The Lord has sworn an oath he will not change.
"You are a priest for ever,
a priest like Melchizedek of old."

The Master standing at your right hand
will shatter kings in the day of his wrath.

He shall drink from the stream by the wayside
and therefore he shall lift up his head.
Glory be...

Psalm 16

Preserve me, God, I take refuge in you.
I say to the Lord: "You are my God.
My happiness lies in you alone".

He has put into my heart a marvellous love
for the faithful ones who dwell in his land.
Those who choose other gods increase their sorrows.
Never will I offer their offerings of blood.
Never will I take their name upon my lips.

O Lord, it is you who are my portion and cup;
it is you yourself who are my prize.
The lot marked out for me is my delight:
welcome indeed the heritage that falls to me!

I will bless the Lord who gives me counsel,
who even at night directs my heart.
I keep the Lord ever in my sight:
since he is at my right hand, I shall stand firm.

And so my heart rejoices, my soul is glad;
even my body shall rest in safety.
For you will not leave my soul among the dead,
nor let your beloved know decay.

You will show me the path of life, the fullness of joy in
your presence, at your right hand happiness for ever.
Glory be...

*(Other psalms suitable for Evening Prayer include psalms 72,
111, 126 & 127.)*

Scripture Reading

Let us give thanks to the God and Father of our Lord
Jesus Christ, the merciful Father, the God from
whom all help comes! He helps us in all our troubles,
so that we are able to help those who have all kinds of
troubles, using the same help that we ourselves have
received from God.

(2 Co 1:34)

Magnificat (Gospel Canticle of Mary)

My soul glorifies the Lord,
my spirit rejoices in God, my Saviour.
He looks on his servant in her lowliness;
henceforth all ages will call me blessed.

The Almighty works marvels for me.
Holy his name!
His mercy is from age to age,
on those who fear him.

He puts forth his arm in strength and
scatters the proud-hearted.
He casts the mighty from their thrones
and raises the lowly.

He fills the starving with good things,
sends the rich away empty.

He protects Israel, his servant,
remembering his mercy,
the mercy promised to our fathers,
to Abraham and his sons for ever.
Glory be...

Short Responsory

R. How manifold are your works, O Lord. (Repeat.)

V. In wisdom you have made them all.

R. How manifold are your works, O Lord.

V. Glory be to the Father, and to the Son,
and to the Holy Spirit.

R. How manifold are your works, O Lord.

Intercessions

V. May your kingdom of peace and justice be realised
on earth as in heaven.

R. Lord, hear our prayer.

V. Show yourself to all who seek you in sincerity
of heart.

R Lord, hear our prayer.

V. O Lord Jesus Christ, light of all the nations, shine
upon all those who walk in darkness and in the
shadow of death.

R. Lord, hear our prayer.

V. Be with all those who suffer in body, mind or spirit.

R. Lord, hear our prayer.

V. Show your mercy to the dead, bring them to rejoice
in the company of the Blessed Virgin Mary and all
your saints.

R. Lord, hear our prayer.

Our Father...

Concluding Prayer

Let our evening prayer rise before you like incense, Lord,
and may your blessing shower down upon us:
so that now and forever your grace may heal and save us.
We ask this through our Lord Jesus Christ your Son,
who lives and reigns in the unity of the Holy Spirit,
ever one God, world without end. Amen.

✠ May the Lord bless us, keep us from all evil and bring
us to everlasting life. Amen.

~ Night Prayer ~

This is the Church's final prayer of the day.

V. O God, come to our aid
R. O Lord, make haste to help us.

G lory be to the Father, and to the Son, and to the Holy Spirit, as it was in the beginning, is now and ever shall be, world without end.
Amen. (Alleluia.)

One of the following or another suitable hymn is said:

N ow it is evening; time to cease from labour,
Father, according to thy will and pleasure,
Through the night-season, have thy faithful people
Safe in thy keeping.

Far from our dwellings drive the evil spirits;
Under the shadow of thy wings protect us;
Be thou our guardian through the hours of darkness,
Strong to defend us.

Call we, 'ere sleeping, on the name of Jesus;
Rise we at day-break, strong to serve thee better;
Order our goings, well begun and ended,
All to thy glory.

Fountain of goodness, bless the sick and needy;
Visit the captive, solace the afflicted;
Shelter the stranger, feed your starving children;
Strengthen the dying.

Father, who neither slumberest nor sleepest,
Thou, to whom darkness is as clear as noonday,
Have us this night-time, for the sake of Jesus,
Safe in thy keeping.

Lead, Kindly Light, amidst th'encircling gloom,
Lead thou me on.
The night is dark, and I am far from home,
Lead thou me on.
Keep thou my feet; I do not ask to see
The distant scene; one step enough for me.

I was not ever thus, nor prayed that thou
Shouldst lead me on;
I loved to choose and see my path; but now
Lead thou me on.
I loved the garish day, and, spite of fears,
Pride ruled my will. Remember not past years.

So long thy power hath blest me, sure it still
Will lead me on.
O'er moor and fen, o'er crag and torrent, till
The night is gone,
And with the morn those angel faces smile,
Which I have loved long since, and lost awhile.

The day thou gavest, Lord, is ended,
The darkness falls at thy behest;
To thee our morning hymns ascended,
Thy praise shall sanctify our rest.

We thank thee that thy church, unsleeping,
While earth rolls onward into light,
Through all the world her watch is keeping,
And rests not now by day or night.

As o'er each continent and island
The dawn leads on another day,
The voice of prayer is never silent,
Nor dies the strain of praise away.

The sun that bids us rest is waking
Our brethren 'neath the western sky,

And hour by hour fresh lips are making
Thy wondrous doings heard on high.

So be it, Lord; thy throne shall never,
Like earth's proud empires, pass away:
Thy kingdom stands, and grows forever,
Till all thy creatures own thy sway.

One or both of the following psalms may be said:

Psalm 4

When I call, answer me,
O God of justice;
from anguish you released me,
have mercy and hear me!

How long, you people,
will your hearts be closed,
will you love what is futile
and seek what is false?

It is the Lord who grants favours
to those whom he loves;
the Lord hears me
whenever I call him.

Fear him: do not sin:
ponder on your bed and be still.
Make justice your sacrifice
and trust in the Lord.

"What can bring us happiness?" many say.
Let the light of your face shine on us, O Lord.

You have put into my heart a greater joy than they have
from abundance of corn and new wine.

I will lie down in peace
and sleep comes at once
for you alone,
Lord, make me dwell in safety.

Glory be...

Psalm 133

O come, bless the Lord,
all you who serve the Lord,
who stand in the house of the Lord,
in the courts of the house of our God.

Lift up your hands to the holy place
And bless the Lord through the night.

May the Lord bless you from Sion,
He who made both heaven and earth.

Glory be...

Scripture Reading

Be calm but vigilant, because your enemy the devil is prowling round like a roaring lion, looking for someone to devour. Stand up to him, strong in faith.

(*1 P* 5:89)

Short Responsory

R. Into your hands, Lord, I commend my spirit. (Repeat.)

V. You have redeemed us, Lord God of truth.

R. Into your hands, Lord, I commend my spirit.

V. Glory be to the Father, and to the Son and to the Holy Spirit.

R. Into your hands, Lord, I commend my spirit.

Nunc Dimittis (Gospel Canticle of Simeon)

Ant. Save us, Lord while we are awake; protect us while we are asleep; that we may keep watch with Christ and rest with him in peace. (Alleluia.)

✝ Now, Lord, you have kept your word: let your servant go in peace.

With my own eyes I have seen the salvation which you have prepared in the sight of every people:

A light to reveal you to the nations and the glory of your people Israel.

Glory be...

Ant. Save us, Lord while we are awake; protect us while we are asleep; That we may keep watch with Christ and rest with him in peace. (Alleluia.)

Concluding Prayer

Visit this house, we pray you, Lord; drive far from it all the snares of the enemy; may your holy angels dwell with us and guard us in peace; and may your blessing be always upon us; through Jesus Christ our Lord. Amen.

or:

Lighten our darkness we beseech you O Lord, and by your great mercy defend us from all the perils and dangers of this night; for the love of your only Son, our Saviour Jesus Christ. Amen.

Blessing

May the Lord grant us a quiet night and a perfect end. Amen. May the souls of the faithful departed, through the mercy of God, rest in peace. Amen.

An anthem to the Blessed Virgin Mary is now said. During Ordinary Time the Salve Regina (p. 68). During Eastertide, the Regina Caeli (p. 71).